BUILDING AMERICA'S
DEMOCRACY ™

Tories and Patriots
Neighbors at War

Jeremy Thornton

The Rosen Publishing Group's
PowerKids Press ™
New York

For my wife, Tracee Sioux

Published in 2003 by The Rosen Publishing Group, Inc.
29 East 21st Street, New York, NY 10010

First Edition

Editor: Joanne Randolph
Book Design: Michael J. Caroleo, Mike Donnellan, Michael de Guzman, Colin Dizengoff

Photo Credits: Cover (background) © Arthur D'Arazien/SuperStock; cover (portrait left), p.16 (inset) Emmet Collection, Miriam and Ira D. Wallach Division of Art, Prints, and Photographs, The New York Public Library, Astor, Lenox and Tilden Foundations; cover (portrait right), p. 19 © Red Hill, The Patrick Henry National Memorial; back cover Library of Congress, Prints and Photographs Division; p. 4 Rare Books and Manuscripts, The New York Public Library, Astor, Lenox and Tilden Foundations; p. 7 courtesy of the Massachusetts Historical Society; p. 8 courtesy of the National Portrait Gallery, London; p. 8 (inset top) © CORBIS; p. 8 (inset bottom) The New York Public Library, Astor, Lenox and Tilden Foundations; p. 11 (portrait) courtesy Museum of Fine Arts, Boston, reproduced with permission. © 2000 Museum of Fine Arts, Boston. All Rights Reserved.; p. 11 (inset) Library of Congress, Manuscript Division; p. 12 © National Portrait Gallery, Smithsonian Institution/Art Resource, NY; p. 12 (inset) Map Division, The New York Public Library, Astor, Lenox and Tilden Foundations; p. 15, 16 courtesy Independence National Historical Park; p. 15 (inset) Gage Papers, Clements Library, University of Michigan; p. 20 (left) © Joseph Sohm, Visions of America/CORBIS; p. 20 (right) © Hulton/Archive/Getty Images.

Thornton, Jeremy.
  Tories and patriots : neighbors at war / Jeremy Thornton.
    p. cm. — (Building America's democracy)
  Summary: Describes the American revolution and gives brief biographical sketches of important leaders of the time.
  Includes bibliographical references (p.) and index.
  ISBN 0-8239-6279-2 (lib. bdg.)
  1. United States—History—Revolution, 1775–1783—Social aspects—Juvenile literature. 2. United States—History—Revolution, 1775–1783—Biography—Juvenile literature. 3. Revolutionaries—United States—Biography—Juvenile literature. 4. American loyalists—Biography—Juvenile literature. 5. United States—Politics and government—1775–1783—Juvenile literature. [1. United States—History—Revolution, 1775–1783. 2. Revolutionaries. 3. American loyalists.] I. Title.
  E209 .T48 2003
    973.3—dc21

                                                    2002001802

Manufactured in the United States of America

Contents

Two Sides of the War

The American Revolution (1775–1783) is often described as a war between the American colonies and Britain. However, it was also a **civil war**. Many of the colonists in America did not want to be independent from Britain. The colonists who sided with Britain were called loyalists, because they stayed loyal to King George III. Loyalists were also called **Tories**. Many other Americans in 1775 were unhappy with Britain's rule. They wanted to have their own government. They called themselves patriots or **Whigs**, but the British called them rebels. Each colonist had to decide which side he would fight for in the war. Neighbors and family members often fought against each other to support the side in which they believed.

On December 16, 1774, colonists dressed as Native Americans dumped 342 boxes of tea into Boston Harbor to protest a British tax on tea.

Independence or Loyalty?

Patriots felt that they had many reasons to seek freedom. The colonies had no **representation** in **Parliament**. As a result, the patriots felt that the British were not interested in the colonists' concerns. Britain passed many new laws in the 1760s and 1770s that increased the amount of taxes the colonists had to pay. Most of the colonists were unhappy about this. They decided to break free of Britain's control.

Loyalists decided not to fight against Britain. Some of them felt the colonists had no chance of winning a war against Britain. Other loyalists made a lot of money trading with Britain. They did not want to lose that money. Some were against the Revolution for **philosophical** reasons.

The snake cut in pieces on this masthead by Paul Revere shows that patriots felt it was important for the colonies to unite if they wanted to fight Britain successfully.

THE Massachusetts Spy

Or, Thomas's Boston Journal.

Do THOU *Great* LIBERTY *inspire our Souls—And make our Lives in* THY *Possession happy—Or, our Deaths glorious in* THY *just Defence.*

VOL. IV.)   THURSDAY, JULY 7, 1774.   (NUMB. 179.

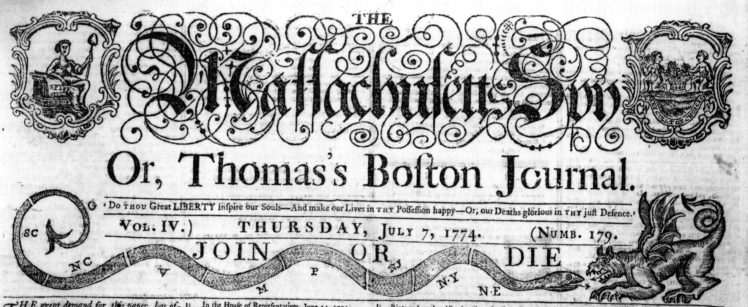

JOIN OR DIE

THE great demand for this paper, has often occasioned many good customers being disappointed, for which the publisher is very sorry: He will, in future, endeavour to prevent any thing of the like kind happening, so long as he may have the honour of being an hand-servant to the public.

The gloomy prospect of public affairs, at present, in this devoted capital, has occasioned some pressing Demands upon him, which with great reluctance he informs his customers, he can by no means answer without their kind assistance: He is loath to trouble them with a

In the House of Representatives, June 14, 1774.

WHEREAS there will become due in this month, sundry notes given by the province-treasurer, and sufficient provision having been made for the paying off the same, and if the possessors of such notes should not bring them in to the treasurer to be paid, the province will suffer damage by such neglect:

Therefore Resolved, That the possessors of such notes, who shall not bring them to the province-treasurer, to be paid by the last day of July next, shall not receive any interest on the same, after that time, and the province treasurer, is hereby directed forthwith to cause this order to be published in all the Boston News-papers, three weeks successively, that every one concerned may be notified hereof.

Sent up for concurrence.   T. CUSHING, speaker
In council, June 15th,   Read and concurred.
     JOHN COTTON, D. sec'ry.

·Riots and weak publications, by a small number of individuals, are sufficient reasons with Parliament to ruin many thousand inhabitants of a truly respectable town, to dissolve charters, to abolish the benefits of the writ of *habeas corpus*,§ and extirpate American liberty—for the principle reaches all. But in *England* the press groans with publications, seditious, treasonable and even blasphemous. The discontented swarm over the kingdom, proclaiming their resentments. Many enormous riots have disturbed the public peace. The sovereign has been insulted in passing from his palace to the Parliament-house, on the business of the nation. Is it to be concluded from these facts, that the BODY OF THE PEOPLE is seditious and traiterous? can his Majesty believe, that he is thought by his English subjects in *general* to be such a prince, as some of them have represented him? will the two houses of Parliament acknowledge what has been spoken and written and acted

adversus validissimas gentis pro nobis utilius, quam quod in COMMUNE NONCONSULUNT. Rarus ad propulsandum *commune periculum* conventus. Ita dum *singuli pugnant omnes vincuntur.*‡

Why did the little *Swiss* cantons, and seven small provinces of the low countries, so successfully oppose the tyrants, that not contended with an empire founded in humanity and mutual advantages, *unnecessarily* and arrogantly strove to " LAY" the faithful and affectionate wretches " AT THEIR FEET?" Because, they wisely regarded the interest of each as the interest of all.

Our own experience furnishes a mournful additional proof of an observation made by a great and good man, Lord president *Forbes.* " It is a certain truth," says he, " that all states and kingdoms, in proportion as they grow great, wealthy and powerful, grow wanton, wicked and oppressive, and the history of all ages gives evidence of the fatal catastrophe

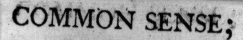

COMMON SENSE;

ADDRESSED TO THE

INHABITANTS

OF

AMERICA,

On the following interesting

SUBJECTS.

I. Of the Origin and Design of Government in general,
with concise Remarks on the English Constitution.

II. Of Monarchy and Hereditary Succession.

III. Thoughts on the present State of American Affairs.

IV. Of the present Ability of America, with some mis-
cellaneous Reflections.

Man knows no Master save creating HEAVEN,
Or those whom choice and common good ordain.

THOMSON.

PHILADELPHIA;

Printed, and Sold, by R. BELL, in Third-Street.

ROB
Price
those who buy per the hundred

PLAIN TRUTH; addressed to the INHA-
BITANTS of AMERICA, containing Remarks
on a late Pamphlet intituled COMMON SENSE.
Wherein are shewn, that the Scheme of INDEPEND-
ENCE is Ruinous, Delusive, and impracticable:
That were the Author's Asseverations, respecting
the Power of AMERICA, as Real as Nugatory, Re-
conciliation, on liberal Principles with GREAT-
BRITAIN would be exalted Policy: And that, cir-
cumstanced as we are, permanent Liberty, and true
Happiness can only be obtained by Reconciliation
with that Kingdom. Written by CANDIDUS.
Will ye turn from Flattery and attend to this side?
There Truth, unlicenc'd, walks; and dares accost
Even Kings themselves, the Monarchs of the Free!
Thompson on the Liberties of Britain.
N. B. To this Pamphlet is subjoined a Defence of
the Liberty of the Press, by the sagacious and pa-
triotic JUNIUS, Author of the celebrated FREE
to his present Majesty, and his Ministers,

Thomas Paine moved to Philadelphia in 1774.

Pamphlet-Writing

Early in the war, many people had not decided whether they wanted to be for or against the Revolution. In January 1776, a British writer named Thomas Paine published a **pamphlet** called *Common Sense* to help people decide. He wrote that Americans had a right to independence and that people should have a say in their government. *Common Sense* convinced many people to join the Revolution.

In March 1776, James Chalmers wrote a response to *Common Sense* called *Plain Truth*. A rich farmer living in Maryland, he wrote *Plain Truth* using the fake name Candidus. Chalmers listed reasons for the colonies to remain loyal to Britain. Chalmers's pamphlet was not nearly as successful as *Common Sense*.

Top left: Common Sense was a best-selling pamphlet. *Bottom left:* This advertisement ran for *Plain Truth,* which supported loyalty to Britain.

Two Sons of Liberty

The Sons of Liberty was a secret group of patriots who fought against the British government and **protested** its decisions. Paul Revere and Benjamin Church were two members of the group. Paul Revere was a **silversmith** living in Boston, Massachusetts. On the night of April 18, 1775, he rode his horse toward Lexington, Massachusetts. On the way, he stopped to warn the colonists that the British army was coming. As a result, the colonists were ready to fight when the British soldiers arrived. Benjamin Church pretended to be a patriot, but he was a spy for the British general Thomas Gage. In return for money, Church gave Gage letters with American military secrets. Church was caught in 1777, and put in prison.

Paul Revere is holding a teapot he made in his silversmith shop. *Inset:* This letter from Benjamin Church is written in code, or a secret system of letters or symbols.

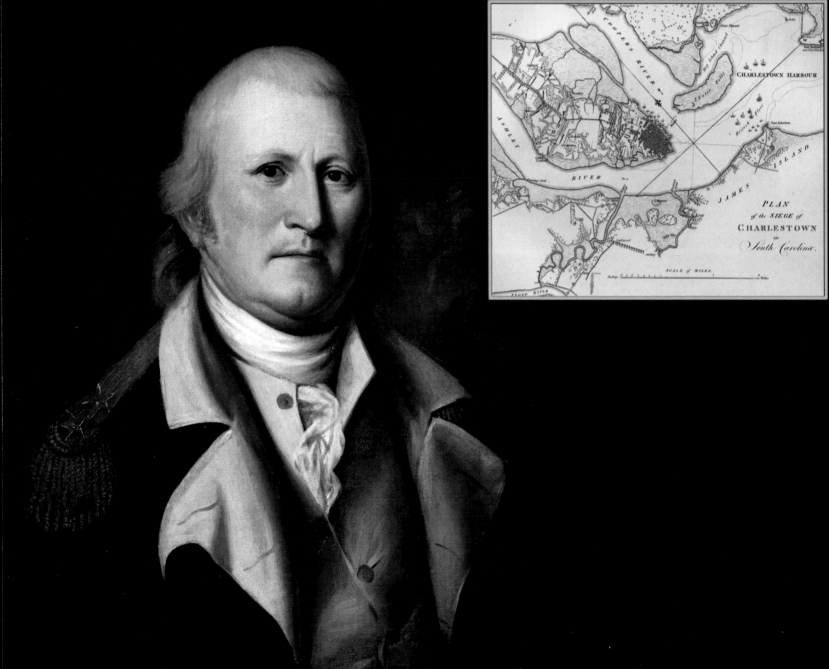

Two Military Historians

Some soldiers wrote down what they saw during the war. This has helped people to learn about history. Anthony Allaire was a lieutenant in the **Loyal American Regiment**. He wrote a diary of the battles in which he fought, including the Battle of Kings Mountain, in Tennessee, and a battle in Charleston, South Carolina. His diary is an important record of the loyalists' side of the American Revolution.

The patriots also had recorders of history. William Moultrie joined the Continental army in 1776. He wrote an account of the American Revolution and how it affected Georgia, North Carolina, and South Carolina. He wrote it using letters and stories that he had written during the war.

A planter from South Carolina, William Moultrie was made a general after he fought bravely in the Battle of Sullivan's Island, at Charleston, South Carolina.

Two Scientists

Scientists or inventors often served as leaders. Such was the case with Benjamin Thompson and Benjamin Franklin. They were politically active during the Revolution. Thompson experimented with gunpowder, folding beds, and moon observation among other things. He served the British government as **undersecretary** of the colonies and later commanded British troops against the patriots.

Benjamin Franklin, a scientist and an inventor, worked hard for the American cause. He was one of the **delegates** to the Continental Congress. He also tried to talk other European countries into supporting the Americans in the war. He invented bifocals, a stove, and many more things.

At first Benjamin Franklin tried to solve the problems with the British government. *Inset:* Benjamin Thompson, a spy, wrote this secret letter in special ink over a normal letter.

Woburn, May 6th 1775

Sir, In compliance with your desires I embrace this first opportunity that has offered since I left Boston to send you some account of the situation of affairs in this part of the Country.

If you will be so kind as to deliver to _____ of Boston, the Papers which I left in your care and take his Receipt for the same, you will much oblige.

I need not trouble you with a particular account of the affair at Concord on Wednesday the 19th Ult. nor the subsequent gathering at Cambridge &c. you have doubtless already better inteligence of them affairs than I am able to give you.

Your Humble Servant

The only information that I can give you that can be of any consequence ___ lately received Saturday May 6 1775 from a Field officer in the Rebel Army (if that mass of confusion may be called an Army) & from a member of the Provincial Congress that is now setting at Watertown. By them I learn that an Army consisting of 30,000 effective men is speedily to be raised in the four New England Governments, & that the quota for this Province is 13,600. That as soon as this Army shall be raised & regulated it is ___ly supposed that the first movement ___ to make a feint attack upon the Town ___ & at the same time to attempt the ___ly the main body of their Army ___ will be the precise plan of ope...

Tory and Patriot Newspapers

During the Revolution, many colonists gave their opinions about the war by writing newspaper articles, such as "Letters of a Westchester Farmer." Samuel Seabury wrote these letters under the pen name "A Westchester Farmer." In the letters, he pretended to be a farmer affected by the war, and he urged people to remain loyal to the king.

Alexander Hamilton, a young patriot, wrote responses to Seabury's letters, arguing the patriot cause. In his letters to the newspaper he signed his name, "A Friend to America." Alexander Hamilton would use newspapers throughout the war, and even after it ended, to argue and to explain his opinions to the American people.

Hamilton's arguments helped to convince people to support the patriots' cause.
Inset: In his letters, Seabury pretended to be a farmer, but he was a wealthy minister.

Tory and Patriot Lawyers

Lawyers are often talented public speakers. During the Revolution, some lawyers argued about the relationship of the colonies to Britain. Patrick Henry was a lawyer from Virginia. He felt it was wrong for the British government to tax the colonies. He called on the colonists to fight against Britain when he said, "Give me liberty, or give me death."

Joseph Galloway was a lawyer from Pennsylvania. He served in the Continental Congress and was one of the most important **spokesmen** for the loyalists. He wanted the colonies to have more freedom, but still be ruled by the king. Congress voted against his "A Plan for the Union of Great Britain and the Colonies," but the plan was only one vote short of being passed.

In this painting, Patrick Henry is speaking against the Stamp Act. The Stamp Act required that the colonists purchase stamps and place them on all printed material.

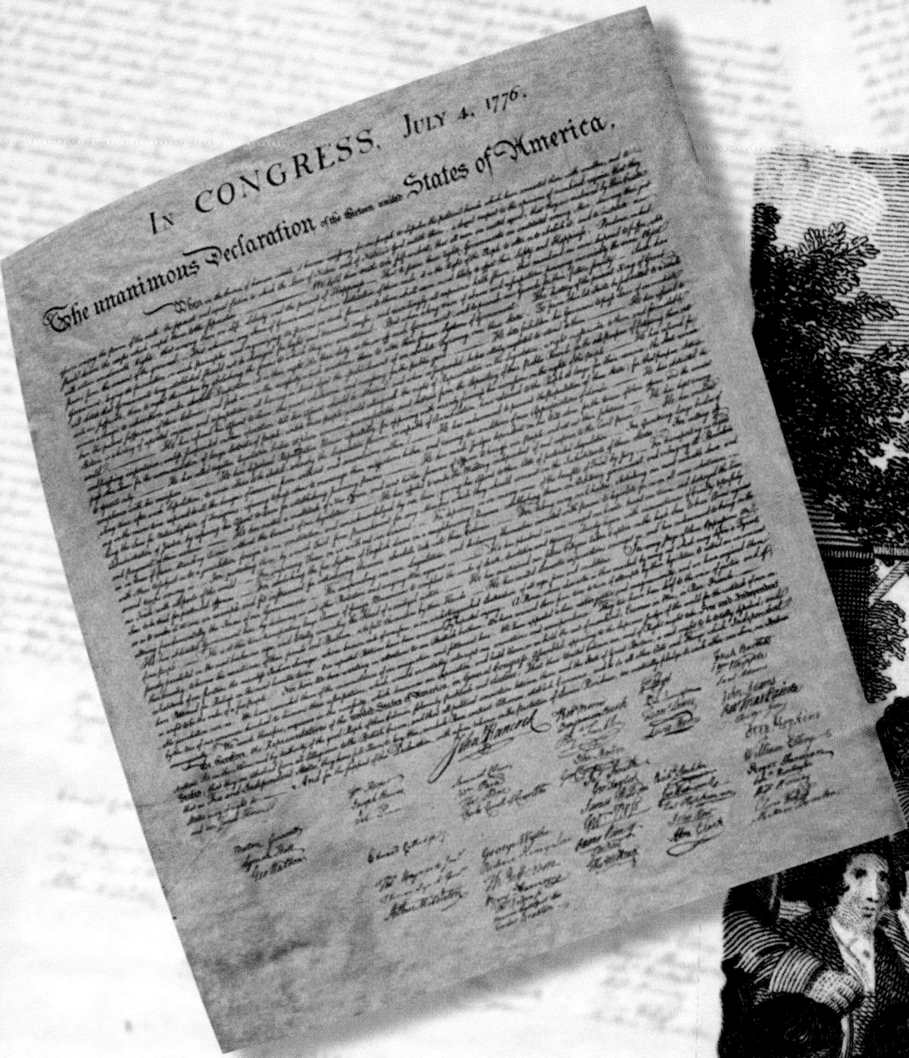
IN CONGRESS, JULY 4, 1776.
The unanimous Declaration of the thirteen united States of America,

Revolutionary Papers

On July 4, 1776, the American patriots published the Declaration of Independence. The patriots wrote that the government should protect the people's freedom, and they listed their complaints against King George III. Finally, they declared themselves independent from British control.

Not all of the colonists agreed with these words. The loyalists did not want to be free from Britain, and they felt it was not right to try to break away. A group of 200 loyalists in New York wrote an answer to the Declaration of Independence. On November 28, 1776, they issued their Declaration of Dependence. In their document, they declared that they would remain loyal to the king.

Left: In the Declaration of Independence, the patriots wrote that all people have the right to "life, liberty, and the pursuit of happiness." *Right:* Patriots punish a loyalist.

Patriots Win

The war ended when Britain and the United States signed a peace agreement called the Treaty of Paris, in 1783. The patriots had succeeded in their struggle. They had won their freedom. They quickly began to work on forming a new government.

The loyalists also had worked and fought hard, but their efforts were not successful. After the war's end, some of the loyalists left America. Many of them went to live in Canada or Britain. Some of them accepted their defeat and stayed in America. Those that remained were examples of the fact that America can be home to many different people, even if they disagree.

Glossary

civil war (SIH-vul WOR) A war between two sides within one country.

delegates (DEH-lih-gets) People who present ideas on behalf of many people.

lawyers (LOI-yerz) Experts who give advice about the law and who represent people in court.

Loyal American Regiment (LOY-ul uh-MER-ih-kin REH-jih-ment) A military group that remained loyal to the British king in the American Revolution.

pamphlet (PAM-flit) An unbound printed publication with no cover or with a paper cover.

Parliament (PAR-lih-mint) The group in Britain that makes the country's laws.

philosophical (fih-luh-SAH-fih-kul) Based on a theory underlying or regarding a sphere of activity or thought.

protested (PROH-test-ed) Objected or gestured in disapproval.

representation (reh-prih-zen-TAY-shun) The act of speaking in the place of or for someone else, usually by legal right.

silversmith (SIHL-ver-smith) Someone who makes crafts and jewels out of silver.

spokesmen (SPOHKS-min) People who talk to the public to give the views of a group.

Tories (TOR-eez) Colonists who were loyal to the British government and wanted to remain under the rule of Britain.

undersecretary (uhn-dur-SEH-kruh-tehr-ee) A secretary immediately subordinate to a principal secretary, or second in charge.

Whigs (WIGZ) Colonists who believed the British were treating the colonies unfairly, and who wanted independence from Britain.

Index

Primary Sources

Cover. Background image: *Battle at Lexington*. This Amos Doolittle portrait done in 1775 based on eyewitness accounts collected by the artist is held at the Concord Art Museum. **Page 7.** *Massachusetts Spy, or Thomas's Boston Journal*, Vol. IV, July 7, 1774 issue. Paul Revere engraved the masthead of this issue. Each segment of the snake is labeled with one of the colony's names. The winged lion, or gryphon, represents the king of Britain. The drawing has the words Join or Die engraved above the snake. This is meant to be a warning to the colonists, that as a snake in pieces is not dangerous, their rebellion will have no effect unless they unite in their fight against Britain. **Page 8.** *Thomas Paine*. This 1880 painting of Paine is by Auguste Milliere, from an engraving by William Sharp, based on George Romney's 1793 portrait. The Milliere portrait is held at the National Portrait Gallery in London. *Right*: This is the title page of the first edition of Thomas Paine's *Common Sense*. It was printed in 1776, by Robert Bell on Third Street in Philadelphia. One hundred fifty thousand copies (equivalent to around fifteen million copies today) were circulating within three months. *Left*: Advertisement for the pamphlet *Plain Truth*. The ad first ran in the March 16 edition of the loyalist newspaper, the *Pennsylvania Ledger*. The pamphlet was also printed by Robert Bell in Philadelphia. The ad offered a bulk discount for those buying per the hundred or dozen. Pamphlet writing was a common way to voice dissent against social or religious injustices as early as the 1500s. **Page 11.** *Paul Revere*. This well-known oil painting of Paul Revere was painted by John Singleton Copley around 1768. Rather than showing Paul Revere in fine clothes as is traditionally done in portraits, Copley has captured an artisan in his natural setting. This painting reflects the simplicity of Revere's life and his pride in his work. This oil portrait is held by the Museum of Fine Arts in Boston. *Inset: Benjamin Church Jr. to Maurice Cane, July, 1775, in code*. This letter is from the George Washington Papers at the Library of Congress. Spy's letters were common at this time. Some used code, some used invisible ink. **Page 12.** *Major General William Moultrie*. This oil portrait was painted in 1782 by Charles Willson Peale. It is currently held at the National Portrait Gallery, Smithsonian Institution. *Inset: Plan of the Siege of Charlestown in South Carolina, 1787*. This map is held at The New York Public Library. **Page 15.** *Benjamin Franklin*. This oil portrait by Joseph Wright was painted around 1782 and is held at the The Corcoran Gallery of Art in Washington, D.C. *Inset: Letter from Benjamin Thompson to unidentified person*. This letter, written by Thompson on May 6, 1775, was written in invisible ink under a visible letter. It is part of the Clements Library, University of Michigan, collection. **Page 16.** *Alexander Hamilton*. This oil portrait was painted by Charles Willson Peale circa 1791. **Page 19.** *Patrick Henry Before the Virginia House of Burgesses*. This 1851 painting by Peter F. Rothermel is held at Red Hill, the Patrick Henry National Memorial. Patrick Henry is presenting his resolutions against the Stamp Act. **Page 20.** *An English sympathiser is strung up and ridiculed by his Patriot neighbours during the American Revolution*. This engraving done around 1776 was printed in famous artist John Trumbull's 1782 book of satirical poems called *M'Fingal*. *Inset: Declaration of Independence*. Library of Congress.

Web Sites

Due to the changing nature of Internet links, PowerKids Press has developed an online list of Web sites related to the subject of this book. This site is updated regularly. Please use this link to access the list:
www.powerkidslinks.com/bad/torpat/